# OUT OF THE EATER
# CAME FORTH MEAT!

# OUT OF THE EATER CAME FORTH MEAT!

DR. DARRELL TOLBERT

**CITIOFBOOKS, INC.**
3736 Eubank NE Suite A1
Albuquerque, NM 87111-3579
*www.citiofbooks.com*
Hotline:      1 (877) 389-2759
Fax:          1 (505) 930-7244

Ordering Information:
Quantity Sales. Special discounts are available on quantity purchases by corporations, associations, and others. For details, contact the publisher at the address above.

Printed in the United States of America.

ISBN-13              Paperback      978-1-959682-10-3
                     eBook          978-1-959682-11-0

Library of Congress Control Number: 2022919444

# INTRODUCTION

In the beginning this world was without form. Void and darkness covered or ruled this world. This world was chaotic. The first thing we see God doing to a world that's chaotic and full of darkness is bringing order. Our God is not a God of chaos; he is a God of divine order!

Darkness is now ruling. In order to establish order, Genesis 1:3 records God in action:

*God said, "Let there be light!"*

When light appears, darkness must disappear! What God is saying to darkness is "Let me establish myself, let me establish my presence, and let me establish my rule and dominion over everything including the kingdom of darkness!"

When darkness had taken over the most prized angel called Lucifer, the shiny one, he rebelled against the all-powerful light. He then spread his darkness over heaven recruiting a third of the angels, thus establishing the kingdom of darkness. There was a war in heaven. Michael (Jesus) and his angels (the kingdom of light) fought against Lucifer (dragon) and his angels (the kingdom of darkness), and the kingdom of light prevailed!

The kingdom of darkness was kicked out of heaven to this earth without form and void, and darkness ruled. God created man and placed him in the middle of a battlefield. Eve allowed darkness to invade her mind by listening to the ruler of darkness. She then spread the darkness to the ruler of this earth Adam through the forbidden fruit. He was the one placed here as a representative of the kingdom of light. Because he loved darkness (thou shalt have no other gods before me), his wife more than he loved God (light) at that particular moment, he rebelled against the kingdom of light and joined the kingdom of darkness, thus sending darkness through him and his seed until the end of time—only to be set free by the arrival of the prince of peace, the one in whom there is no darkness, the one whose presence lights the whole world, Jesus the only begotten son of God.

The stage is now set. The battle between light and darkness will no longer just include the spiritual realm. It will be carried out in the physical realm also. The children of the kingdom of light will battle against the children of the kingdom of darkness. Make no mistake about it. There is no neutral ground on this planet called Earth. You are fighting with the kingdom of light or fighting against it. Those who aren't for Jesus are against him; those who aren't saved are on the side of the kingdom of darkness with Satan as their god and ruler.

This battle is real, death is real, and both kingdoms have power to kill, bless, and curse. Contrary to belief, the kingdom of darkness is not powerless. Its power is controlled by the one who has all power—the one who sits in the middle seat position of his throne, the creator and ruler of the whole universe, the Father Elohim (self-existing one or one who exists outside of self). Under the control of the Father, the stage is set. The children of the kingdom of light and the children of the kingdom of darkness are now engaged in a heated life-or-death battle.

# OUT OF THE EATER
# CAME FORTH MEAT!

When God delivered his people from under the bondage and rulership of Pharoah in the nation of Egypt, he directed them toward a promise land—a land flowing with milk and honey, with houses which they did not build (the wealth of the wicked; the kingdom of darkness is laid up for the children of the kingdom of light), cattle which they did not feed, and vineyards and crops which they did not plant. Even though this land had been promised, a battle must take place. It was occupied by the children of the kingdom of darkness. As seen in the deliverance of God's people from Egypt, the devil fought to hold on to that which he deemed as his. Not only he fought to keep it, after it had been freed from his grips. He pursued and tried to recapture it with relentless evil—even if it meant destruction to his followers as seen in the mad pursuit of Pharoah and his army which perished in the Red Sea!

> And it was told the king of Egypt that the people fled: and the heart of Pharaoh and of his servants was turned against the people, and they said, "Why have we done this, that we have let Israel go from serving us?"
> And he made ready his chariot, and took his people with him.
> And he took six hundred chosen chariots, and all the chariots of Egypt, and captains over every one of them.
> And the Lord hardened the heart of Pharaoh king of Egypt, and he pursued after the children of Israel: and the children of Israel went out with a high hand.
> But the Egyptians pursued after them, all the horses and chariots of Pharaoh, and his horsemen, and his army, and

*overtook them encamping by the sea, beside Pi-hahiroth, before Baal-zephon. (Exodus 14:5–9)*

*And Moses stretched out his hand over the sea; and the Lord caused the sea to go back by a strong east wind all that night, and made the sea dry land, and the waters were divided.*

*And the children of Israel went into the midst of the sea upon the dry ground; and the waters were a wall unto them on their right hand, and on their left.*

*And the Egyptians pursued, and went in after them to the midst of the sea, even all Pharaoh's horses, his chariots, and his horsemen.*

*And it came to pass, that in the morning watch the Lord looked unto the host of the Egyptians through the pillar of fire and of the cloud, and troubled the host of the Egyptians.*

*And took off their chariots wheels, that they drave them heavily: so that the Egyptians said, "Let us flee from the face of Israel"; for the Lord fighteth for them against the Egyptians.*

*And the Lord said unto Moses, "Stretch out thine hand over the sea, that the waters may come again upon the Egyptians, upon their chariots, and upon their horsemen."*

*And Moses stretched forth his hand over the sea, and the sea returned to his strength when the morning appeared; and the Egyptians fled against it; and the Lord overthrew the Egyptians in the mist of the sea.*

*And the waters returned, and covered the chariots, and the horsemen, and all the host of Pharaoh that came into the sea after them; there remained not so much as one of them. (Exodus 14: 21–28)*

This land is filled with giants and warriors ready to fight to their death, nations stronger and bigger in the physical but far weaker spiritually. In fact, they are dead in their trespasses and sins. God is a God of love and mercy. As a result of this love and mercy, his nature demands that he punish the evildoer. First is with a rod of correction which is designed to correct the disobedience and push the person closer to God or turn their attention to God. God never punishes without warnings first. Second is the punishment of destruction which can be fatal to those who refuse the punishment of correction.

We all have a cup which slowly fills up with blanket disregard to the warnings of God. Once filled to the top, judgment follows. Genesis 15:13–16 reads:

> *And he said unto Abram, "Know of a surety that thy seed shall be a stranger in a land that is not theirs, and shall serve them; and they shall afflict them four hun-dred years.*
> *And also that nation, whom they shall serve, will I judge: and afterward shall they come out with great substance.*
> *And thou shalt go to thy fathers in peace; thou shalt be buried in a good old age.*
> *But in the fourth generation they shall come hither again:* For the iniquity of the Amorites is not yet full (emphasis added)."

God told Abram that "Yes, I am the one that is going to allow your seed to be in bondage for this amount of time, four hundred years."

This makes me want to shout because it's telling me that my tribulations have an ending point set by God. When he brings me out, I come out with great substance—a deeper and more richer relationship with the Father, wisdom that can only be gained by being in a tribulation! Amen, somebody!

He said, "I am watching the wickedness of the Amorites. Their cup is filling up. It's not full yet, but by the time I deliver my people from bondage, it will be full and I will lead my people back to the land you are in to punish them for their sins!"

From the time God spoke to Abram, the Amorites had at least six hundred or more years to get it right. What a God of love and compassion we serve!

Why did he delay punishment for so long? It is not in God's will that any should perish, but He calls all men to repentance. The stage is set. Moses and the children of the Most High God began to walk into the promises of God by driving out the enemy before them. This is powerful because God has promised us many things, but sometimes in order to receive them, we must do battle with the thing or people holding them captive! The majority of the time I have to do battle within my own self because my greatest enemy is the old man that's dying within me. We like to cast the blame on the prince of the power of the air, but the truth of the matter is we are held captive because we enjoy the sweetness of sin which in time sours in our mouth.

As Moses and the children of Israel advanced on faith toward their new home, God gave a promise to them in Deuteronomy 7:22:

> *The Lord your God will clear away these nations before you little by little. You may not make an end of them at once, lest the wild beasts grow too numerous for you.*

Even though God had promised them victory, he did not drive out or destroy all the nations at once. Had he done this as they drove one nation out after another, in their absence of the vacant cities, wild animals would have moved in and made the cities their homes causing Israel to have to do battle again with the wild animals to drive them out when it was time to inhabit the city. When God delivers us from one stronghold or bad habit, it must be replaced with a good one.

I am excited over this illumination because it shows me as a believer that even though God has promised total deliverance over my sins and strongholds, he will not do it all at once in the physical realm because if he did, I won't pray like I should, I won't come to church like I should, I won't read my Bible like I should, and I won't call on the name of Jesus like I should. God allows some struggles to keep me close to him. It's in the struggles that I learn whom God is. It's in these struggles God stops being just the name God and becomes my Abba Father, my daddy! King David said it best.

He said, "I was glad because I was afflicted. In my affliction I have learned the statutes of God. A caterpillar goes into a cocoon, and a changing effect takes place."

A struggle takes place as he tries to free himself. If you cut the cocoon to free him of his struggles, he comes out deformed, with wings undeveloped. The good that you thought you were doing by easing a person's struggles could cause them to be spiritually unde-veloped. It's the struggle that causes the new formed butterfly wings to harden and form in such a way that they will now take him to unknown heights, higher than he ever thought possible because as a worm he could only look up and wish. As a worm, he could only crawl through the muck and mire; but unknown to the worm, brighter days were ahead. One day, something triggers inside of him and he begins to spin a cocoon.

Metamorphosis takes place (a changing effect) when he comes forth after the struggle. He is no longer the same; he has been given a new name. When his old name worm is mentioned, most run from him or draw back. Some look upon him in disgust because nobody wanted to be close to a worm. But the worm has a new name; he is now called a butterfly. No longer do people run from him, but they run toward him. No longer is there a look of disgust when they see him, but a look of delight and admiration. We all were that worm, born a sinner! No power over sin, we were crawling through the pol-lution of sin in this world.

But one day I believed the gospel, and a changing effect took place—a new name was given! A struggle took place, and because God allowed and ordained the struggle, I developed into a mature sheep, joint heir, wheat, ambassador, Christian, etc. Thank God for the struggle! Moses and the old generation died in the wilderness, and only Joshua and the new or young generation entered the prom-ise land. It is symbolic that the old man inside of me cannot enter into the kingdom of heaven. It's the new man that will enter into the kingdom of heaven. The promises of God are given to the new man (creation), but the problem is this: Too many people are still living in the old man trying to claim the promises for the new man!

Everybody wants to go to heaven, but most aren't willing to pay the price it takes to get there! The price is not money because if heaven was a thing money could buy, the rich would live and the poor would die. This price everybody can pay. It's death to oneself. It's taking the crown off my head as lord, ruler, and king over my life and putting it on the head of the one true king, Jesus, thus making him lord, ruler, and king over my life. Paul said it best when he said for me to die is gain!

Then he also said, "It's no longer I that lives but rather Christ that lives in me!"

The Bible is clear that as a disciple of Jesus, I must take up my cross daily. The thing most believers fail to comprehend is that the cross is an instrument of *death* and *pain*!

When I nail my hands to the cross, it's symbolic that I have surrendered my will. I have given up trying to provide for myself. I am now relying on the promises of my Father—"I will take care of all your needs according to my riches in glory." When I nail my feet to the cross, it's symbolic that I no longer try to find my own way because there is a way that seems right unto a man, but that way is a way to destruction. I no longer go to places I shouldn't go; the Lord is now my shepherd. He leads and guides me; his word is a lamp unto my feet illuminating the steps and direction in which I should go. No longer do my feet tread through darkness but steady forward on the path of righteousness, surrounded by light toward heaven!

Moses sent out twelve spies to spy out the land. Ten came back with a bad report of unbelief and two with a report of faith in the promise of God concerning victory over all their enemies. Numbers 13:25–33 reads:

And they returned from searching of the land after forty days.

> *And they went and came to Moses, and to Aaron, and to all the congregation of the children of Israel, unto the wilderness of Paran, to Kadesh; and brought back word unto them, and unto all the congregation, and shewed them the fruit of the land.*
>
> *And they told him, and said, "We came unto the land whither thou sentest us, and surely it floweth with milk and honey; and this is the fruit of it.*
>
> *Nevertheless the people be strong that dwell in the land, and the cities are walled, and very great: and moreover we saw the children of Anak there.*
>
> *The Amalekites dwell in the land of the south: and the Hittites, and the Jebusites, and the Amorites, dwell in the mountains: and the Canaanites dwell by the sea, and by the coast of Jordan."*
>
> *And Caleb stilled the people before Moses, and said, "Let us go up at once, and possess it; for we are well able to overcome it."*
>
> *But the men that went up with him said, "We be not able to go up against the people; for they are stronger than we."*
>
> *And they brought up an evil report of the land which they had searched unto the children of Israel, say-ing, "The land, through which we have gone to search it, is a land*

*that eateth up the inhabitants thereof; and all the people*
*that we saw in it are men of great stature.*
*And there we saw the giants, the sons of Anak, which come*
*of the giants: and we were in our own sight as grasshoppers,*
*and so we were in their sight."*

Moses sent out the twelve, and ten did not understand the mis-sion. They thought the mission was to see if they could take the land. What they failed to realize was that the land was already theirs. The giants had already been defeated and driven out by God! When God speaks a word, it's already done in the spiritual realm. That's why we walk by faith and not by sight. They walked by sight; therefore, they came back with a few of the blessings of the land, but they did not come back with a report of victory. They came back with a report of unbelief that crippled the faith of the others! Joshua and Caleb understood the land belonged to them and the mission was to go walk into the blessings of God! Even though they saw the giants, they knew that they were only temporary, here today but gone tomorrow; therefore, they brought back a report of victory!

They remembered the words of God concerning the killing machines of the soldiers in Pharaoh's army: "These Egyptians you see today, you will see them no more!" The army of Pharaoh which was more powerful and deadly than the giants was destroyed by the Almighty God. If he took care of that problem, surely he will take care of this one. As saints of God, when we face problems, we need to think about past victories God performed for us. These past vic-tories should increase our faith in our Father. If he did it back then, surely he will do it now! Giants by the power of the Holy Ghost do fall if we keep our eyes on the promises instead of the current situation.

Pharaoh's army suffered the wrath of God by drowning. God wanted to show the whole world that this God of Israel was the same God in Noah's days who vented his wrath on the children of disobe-dience and drowned them in the flood—the one and only true God, the Alpha and the Omega, the first and the last! The promise of the land had been given to all. It was now up to the people to choose which report they would believe. The report of the ten or the report of the two. How many times have we been put into that position? When you are a believer in the word of God, the choice really isn't a hard one. Which report lines up with the word of God?

God said, "I have given the land to you!"

We can't take the land that doesn't line up with the spoken word of God. We can take the land that lines up with the spoken word, but the people made the choice to believe the word that didn't line up with the word of God. That spirit of unbelief is still present in the body of Christ today. The people believe everything except what the word says about their situation, thus blocking them from their blessing and sending them back to wander in the wilderness. On the verge of the promise, unbelief sets them back.

God sent them back into the wilderness for forty years until the old generation of unbelief died! God is still leading us through the desert. It's in the desert the old man born from Adam is destroyed. He is the enemy of God! Even though he is yourself, he is still your greatest enemy. He is the enemy of faith, and faith is the substance we need to obtain all the promises of God. He self-destroys the *can-do* spirit and replaces it with the spirit of fear. The can-do spirit says I *can do all things through Christ who strengthens me!* The spirit of fear says I am not educated enough, I can't stand in front of people, I can't speak well enough, I *can't*, I *can't!*

With that mentality, guess what? You won't! Therefore, we are commanded to deny ourselves daily and to crucify the old man. Faith brings victory, but a lack of faith brings defeat! Jesus himself later was led into the wilderness by the Holy Ghost. He demonstrated that being in the desert isn't a place to complain but a place to get closer to God—a place where the old man dies and the new man comes alive. The number 40 means death to the old man and the newest of life. The old man cannot enter into the promises of God; he cannot get into the promise land or heaven. The desert is a dry hot place where you are shut in by God; it is here the purging takes place.

The question now becomes, what's the purpose of the leading of us into the wilderness? Deuteronomy 8:2–3 gives us insight to help answer this question:

> *And thou shalt remember all the way which the Lord thy God led thee these forty years into the wilderness,* to humble thee, *and* to prove thee, *to* know what was

in thine heart, *to* know if thou wouldest keep his commandments, or no (emphasis added).
*And he humbled thee, and suffered thee to hunger, and fed thee with manna, which thou knewest not, neither did thou fathers know; that he might* make thee know that man doeth not live by bread only, but by every word that proceedeth out of the mouth of the Lord doth man live (emphasis added).

When the wilderness has served its God's divine purpose and God is ready to showcase us to the world, we are led out by the Holy Ghost with *power*! Song of Solomon 3:6 paints a beautiful picture of the finished product of the wilderness experience:

*Who is this that cometh out of the wilderness like pillars of smoke, perfumed with* myrrh and frankincense (emphasis added), *with all the powders of the merchants?*

We went into the wilderness with the smell of this dying decay-ing world—a smell of death because the wages of sin is death. But as the result of the desert experience, the Holy Ghost used it to crush that alabaster box God put into our souls the moment we believed on the name of Jesus and made him Lord over us.

We went in the desert stinking, but now we come out smell-ing like a divine fragrance of myrrh! Why the smell of myrrh? It is because myrrh is a very bitter gum resin used for perfume and as part of the *anointing oil.* The wilderness's processing will bring out the sweet fragrance of his nature and remove the stench of our own self-righteousness! Why the smell of frankincense? Frankincense has many purposes, but the one I will focus on is the one for sacrificial fumigation. Dying to self is not easy nor sweet, but God knows what to apply so there are no lingering odors of the flesh.

When the work is finished, there is a return of a people that shall show forth the power and glory of God—the one who is able to resurrect the dead and the one who was able to breathe life into a valley of dry bones and create a mighty Holy Ghost-filled army fit for his glorious use! The old generation under the leadership of Moses had all died out. A new generation under a new leadership of Joshua now stepped into the promise land with power! Moses represents your pastor or leader.

They have the ability to lead you through the desert, but they can't take you to the promise land which represents heaven.

Joshua represents Jesus. Not only is he in the desert with you encouraging you to move forward by faith and claim the promises of God, but he also has the ability to lead you into the promise land of heaven! Battle ready, the children of God moved forward in their divine purpose being the hand of God driving out their enemies before them—reaping the harvest God promised them, occupying houses their hands did not build, and possessing cattle they did not raise and vineyards they did not plant! They were now living in the victory promised to them by the Father. Years passed and the victories were short-lived, Joshua was dead. The warnings given to the people by God soon were ignored.

Another generation had replaced the generation of Joshua and those who first crossed over into the promise land. Judges 2:6–10 records this:

> *And when Joshua had let the people go, the children of Israel went every man unto his inheritance to possess the land.*
> *And the people served the Lord all the days of Joshua, and all the days of the elders who outlived Joshua, who had seen all the great works of the Lord that he did for Israel.*
> *And Joshua the son of Nun, the servant of the Lord, died, being a hundred and ten years old.*
> *And they buried him in the border of his inheritance in Timnath-heres, in the mount of Ephraim, on the north side of the hill Gaash.*
> *And also, all that generation were gathered unto their fathers: and there arose another generation after them, which knew not the Lord, nor yet the works which he had done for Israel.*

God had warned them: *Do not be like the inhabitants of the land which I gave you victory over!* The people of God soon began to wor-ship the pagan gods of the land. They wanted to be like the pagans; they wanted a human king instead of the king of glory. In 2015, I saw that same mentality inside of the church. We want to be like the world. We want their music, their dances, and their dress code. We look to the world for the standard when God set us as representative of his so the world can look to us as the example.

We are the light that God has set upon a hill to be shining into a darken world giving the lost sinner direction to the one who's able to save his soul from a burning hell, one who's able to put his feet upon solid ground, one who's able to transform a sinner into a saint, one who's able to take the sinner's sins and then give the sinner his righteousness, and one who's able to take the sinner's death upon the cross and then give the sinner his life which is eternal life! The command is given by God: *My people, come out from among them, and be you separate from them!* Like the children of Israel, we have ignored the warnings, and destruction will be the same result if this evil is not corrected.

However, before the Jews were given a king, they had judges. The term "judges" refers to those raised up by God to lead his people.

> *And the children of Israel did evil in the sight of the Lord, and served Balaam.*
> *And they forsook the Lord God of their fathers, which brought them out of the land of Egypt, and fol-lowed other gods, of the gods of the people that were round about them, and bowed themselves unto them, and provoked the Lord to anger.*
> *And they forsook the Lord, and served Baal and Ashtaroth.*
> *And the anger of the Lord was hot against Israel, and he delivered them into the hands of the spoilers that spoiled them, and he sold them into the hands of their enemies round about, so that they could not any longer stand before their enemies.*
> *Whithersoever they went out, the hand of the Lord was against them for evil, as the Lord had said, and as the Lord had sworn unto them: and they were greatly distressed.*
> *Nevertheless, the Lord raised up judges, which delivered them out of the hand of those that spoiled them.*
> *And yet they would not hearken unto their judges, but they went a whoring after others god, and bowed themselves unto them: they turned quickly out the way which their*

*fathers walked in, obeying the commandments of the Lord; but they did not so.*

*And when the Lord raised them up judges, then the Lord was with the judge, and delivered them out the hand of their enemies all the days of the judge: for it repented the Lord because of their groaning by reason of them that oppressed them and vexed them.*

*And it came to pass, when the judge was dead, that they returned, and corrupted themselves more than their fathers, in following other gods to serve them, and to bow down unto them; they ceased not from their own doings, nor from their stubborn way. (Judges 2:11–19)*

The first judge rose after Joshua died in 1350 BC. The first judge was Othniel, Caleb's younger brother. Caleb was the one with Joshua who had brought the good report of faith concerning the promise land. The last judges were Samuel and Eli, a total of thirteen judges which judge the children of Israel for 346 years. The one judge that I want to focus on is Samson, the strongest of all the judges physically but not spiritually. Let me give you a little background history on this awesome man of God. I picked Samson because of the hidden foreshadows and symbolic ties to Jesus Christ and the hidden pro-phetic death of Jesus on the cross between two thieves. This story is loaded with hidden diamonds, rubies, onyx, and so many more pre-cious jewels that we shall uncover by the power of the Holy Ghost!

Our Father has promised us that if we seek, we shall find! If we knock, it shall be open unto us!

*And the children of Israel did evil again in the sight of the Lord; and the Lord delivered them into the hand of the Philistines for forty years.*

*And there was a certain man of Zorah, of the family of the Danites, whose name was Manoah; and his wife was barren, and bare not.*

*And the angel of the Lord appeared unto the woman, and said unto her, "Behold now, thou art barren, and bearest not: but thou shalt conceive, and bear a son.*

*Now therefore beware, I pray thee, and drink not wine nor strong drink, and eat not any unclean thing.*
*For, lo, thou shalt conceive, and bear a son; and no razor shall come on his head: for the child shall be a Nazarite unto God from the womb: and he shall begin to deliver Israel out of the hands of the Philistines."*
*Then the woman came and told her husband, say-ing, "A man of God came unto me, and his countenance was like the countenance of an angel of God, very terrible: but I asked him not whence he was, neither told me his name.*
*But he said unto me, 'Behold, thou shalt conceive, and bear a son; and now drink no wine nor strong drink, neither eat any unclean thing; for the child shall be a Nazarite to God from the womb to the day of his death.'"*
*(Judges 13: 1–7)*

Interestingly the angel appeared unto the wife first and gave her instruction concerning how this gift from God should be raised: "Train them up in the way of the Lord, and when they are old they shall not depart from it." The wife then gave the information to her husband, Manoah, which meant rest or a present. Indeed our God will give us peace during our storms in this life. But Manoah didn't take her word for it; he went and inquired of God himself. Let this be a very valuable lesson to all of us. Too many are accepting what a prophet, prophetess, pastor, bishop, apostle, etc. said concerning God's purpose for their lives instead of seeking God to see if indeed it is his will!

The word of God declares, "I will not have you ignorant (lack of knowledge or void of light)."

Too many are in positions in the church out of ignorance. They may be in these positions, but they are not effective due to the fact that God did not call them to operate in that position. Somebody gave them a prophecy, and based on that they assumed it was their divine purpose. Paul said that we all must abide in our own calling! Paul understood that whom God calls he also equips—meaning there is an anointing which is a power source to empower you to carry out the assignment or position God has sent you into the earth to operate in.

One of the major problems in the church is the believers do not know their divine purpose. They confuse their job which is their necessity with their divine purpose which God anointed them to do. I am a truck driver which is my necessity. It pays my bills and pro-vides for my necessities in this life. My purpose is to pastor and teach the people of God. I am not anointed to drive a semi-truck. It's a skill that can be perfected through years of experience; however, I am anointed to pastor and teach the gospel of God for the edification of the church.

The problem in a lot of churches is that many are in the pulpit out of necessity and not out of a divine purpose! Trust me there is a big difference between the two! They are after the money and fame without the anointing which breaks every chain! The word of God is clear: It's not the whooping or hollering or the huh or haw which breaks the yoke, but it's the anointing that breaks the yoke! We should seek the face of God through fasting and prayer for the divine purpose in which he sent us into this dying and sin-afflicted world. Do not allow people to tell you what God himself will tell you. People can only affirm what God has already showed you through his word or dreams.

God granted the request, and the angel appeared unto the wife again. She ran and got Manoah. Manoah ran after her, and the angel told him the same instructions he had previously told his wife. Many are under the understanding that Jesus's first appearance of this earth was as a baby, but many scriptures show him being here in human form or a form of an angel. This man in the form of an angel is Jesus. How do I know? It is because of the name he gave Manoah in the request to know his name.

> And Manoah said unto the angel of the Lord, "What is thy name, that when thy saying comes to pass we may do thee honor?"
> And the angel of the Lord said unto him, "Why askest thou thus after my name, seeing it is secret (emphasis added)?
> (Judges 13: 17–18)

If you looked up the Hebrew word for secret (pali 6383), you will find it's an improper translation and should be translated as *wonder* which is an adjectival form of the noun peli (6382), which occurs in the Messianic prophecy in Isaiah 9:6–7 which reads:

> For unto us a child is born, unto us a son is given: and the government shall be upon his shoulder: and his name

*shall be called Wonderful, Counselor, The Mighty God, The Everlasting Father, The Prince of Peace.*
*Of the increase of his government and peace there shall be no end, upon the throne of David, and upon his kingdom, to order it, and to establish it with judgment and with justice from henceforth even forever. The zeal of the Lord of hosts will perform this.*

In the study of Samson's life, we will see that he is a symbolic Jesus Christ both on the same mission to free the Father's people from their bondage and oppressors. Let's look as Judges 13:19–22 reads:

*So Manoah took a kid with a meat offering, and offered it upon a rock* (emphasis added) *unto the Lord: and the angel did wondrously; and Manoah and his wife looked on.*
*For it came to pass, when the flame went up toward heaven from off the altar, that the angel of the Lord ascended in the flame of the altar. And Manoah and his wife looked on it, and fell on their faces to the ground.*
*But the angel of the Lord did no more appear to Manoah and to his wife. Then Manoah knew that he was an angel of the Lord.*
*And Manoah said unto his wife, "We shall surely die, because we have seen God."*

The promised child was born, and he was called by the name of Samson. Throughout the rest of this story on the life of Samson, I will point out the similarities between him and Jesus beginning with his name. The name Samson is a Hebrew baby name. In Hebrew it means sun child or bright sun. Jesus is the son child, the only begot-ten son of the living God!

*For the Lord God is a sun* (emphasis added) *and shield: the Lord will give and glory: no good thing will he with-hold from them that walk uprightly. (Psalms 84:11)*
*But unto you that fear my name shall the Sun of righteousness arise with healing in his wings; and ye shall*

*go forth, and go grow up as calves of the stall. (Malachi 4:2)*

These verses clearly show Jesus hidden inside of Samson. The similarities are undeniable. Both were sent by the Father on the same mission: to deliver God's people out of bondage from the enemy. The angel appeared to the women first in both instances; both women had never conceived a baby before. I will continue to point out these hidden and powerful points as we move forward in this story. Samson was anointed by the Holy Ghost to carry out his mission. Jesus after baptism was anointed by the Holy Ghost to carry out his mission. Whom God calls he also equips. God has never called anybody to carry out a mission for him without giving them everything they need to be successful!

Therefore, we are warned to abide in our own calling. There is no power given for me to do your calling. I am anointed to pastor and teach the gospel. I am successful in those areas because there is a power source that I tap into, and it empowers me to carry out my mission. God has not called me to be a soloist. If I try to operate in that calling, it will end in disaster! lol. Know the reason why God sent you here, abide in it, and success will follow you all the days of your life.

Samson was now a young man in a position to make his own choices in life. I am sure he was raised up by the instructions given to his parents. However, we saw the children of God cohabitating with the enemy, the Philistines. The relationship between the two was made possible with the Philistines operating as the greater nation and the Jews as the lesser. Whenever you as a believer partner up with the unbeliever, normally it's the believer who ends up compromising in his relationship with God in order to maintain his or her relationship with the unbeliever. It is easier for the unbeliever to pull you down than for you to pull them up!

Samson had a desire for the unsaved women. When you operate close to the forbidden, most of the time the forbidden become the object of our desires. He saw a gorgeous woman of the Philistine people.

Even though forbidden, he ran to his parents and said, "I have seen a woman of the Philistines. Get her for me for she *pleases me well!*"

The problem we have as believers is that we focus all our attention and efforts on those things that please us well rather than focusing on all the things that please our Father well. Self-gratification has been the shipwreck and downfall of so many great Christians. We received this from our mother Eve, the pleasure from eating the forbidden fruit. The fig was pleasant to the eye, one to be desired—a desire that went against the desires of God!

She ate, thus joining the kingdom of darkness, and then she presented the forbidden fruit, a fig, to her husband. Sin is not content with just contaminating one person. It wants to contaminate and destroy everybody whom that person comes in contact with.

Adam out of love ate and joined Eve in her rebellion, thus spreading sin through every person who came through the loins of a man.

The woman he desired was from Timnath. Interesting enough, the name has several powerful meanings. The first is *forbidden*, and the second is *assigned portion*. Whatever a man sows, that also shall he reap! When we partake of those things which are forbidden by God, there is an assigned portion of painful consequences that is followed. The Bible is clear that the wages (assigned portion) of sin is death!

Some partake in the forbidden use of drugs. The assigned portion they reap is a life-destroying addiction, which normally consists of stealing, prostitution, robbing, loss of morals, improper hygiene, loss of children, abortions, prisons, jail, hospitals, and eventually if not overcome death! Even sex which is forbidden for those not married and forbidden for those who are married to engage in it outside their marriage comes with an assigned portion—venereal diseases such as aids, herpes, gonorrhea, syphilis, etc. and also unwanted pregnancies, divorces, sexual soulties, sexual addictions, and maybe death. The point here is there is an assigned portion to all of our choices whether good or bad; therefore, choose wisely according to the will of our Father who is in heaven.

The third comes with the suggestion of *withhold* or *restraint*. We all enter this world with an assignment from God. Partaking of that which is forbidden *withholds* or *restrains* us from doing that which God has ordained and empowered us to do. Samson's parents knew that if he marries this forbidden woman, the union will withhold him from his Godly mission; therefore, they protested and suggested women from his own people. I put a portion of the blame that eventually caused the demise of Samson on his parents. They had been given specific instructions from God concerning their son. They knew it's forbidden for them to pay the bride price or also known as the bride wealth to the father of this Philistine woman for a marriage union between their son and her.

Samson protested their decision; his parents gave in to their son. In order to understand why you have to really get into the mindset of his parents, they had wanted a child for so long. Years had gone by and the hope seemed slim to none. Finally the thing they so desperately wanted was granted, a child—not just any child but a male child. Back in those days, a male child was the desire of the parents. A male child was a sign of the continuation of the father's name through his seed. Samson was also the only child; therefore, a hypothesis made by myself would suggest he was spoiled by his parents. He was used to getting his way. Just throw a temper tantrum and his parents would eventually give him that which he desired.

Matthew 10:37 gives us, the believer, a warning concerning our love for others more than our love for our Father.

> *Anyone who loves their father or mother more than me is not worthy of me; anyone who loves their son or daughter more than me is not worthy of me.*

Samson's mother and father loved him more than they loved God, so in spite of knowing they were going against the will of God, they gave in, thus setting up their son on a path that led to his destruction. A major lesson to all parents including myself: *Never compromise the will of God just to please our kids!* The devil will have us thinking we are helping them, but every compromise is hurting not helping them!

> *Then went Samson down, and his father and his mother, to Timnath, and came to the vineyards of Timnath: and behold, a young lion roared against him.*
> *And the spirit of the Lord came mightily upon him, and he rent him as he would rent a kid, and he had nothing in his hand: but he told not his father or his mother what he had done.*
> *And he went down, and talked with the woman; and she pleased Samson well.*

> *And after a time, he returned to take her, and he turned aside to see the carcass of the lion: and, behold, there was a swarm of bees and honey in the carcass of the lion.*
> *And he took thereof in his hands, and went on eating, and came to his father and mother, and he gave them, and they did eat: but he told not them that he had taken the honey out of the carcass of the lion.*
> *So, his father went down unto the woman: and Samson made there a feast; for so used the young men to do.*
> *And it came to pass, when they saw him, that they brought thirty companions to be with him.*
> *And Samson said unto them, I will now put forth a riddle unto you: if ye can certainly declare it to me within the seven days of the feast, and find it out, then I will give you thirty pieces of sheets and thirty change of garments.*
> *But if ye cannot declare it me, then shall ye give me thirty sheets and thirty change of garments. And they said unto him, "Put forth thy riddle, that we may hear it."*
> *And he said unto them, "Out of the eater (hunter) came forth meat, and out of the strong came forth sweetness."*
> *And they could not in three days expound the riddle.*
> *(Judges 14: 5–14)*

Samson encountered a lion; the question now becomes, why did God want us to know about this experience? Proverbs 25:2 will help give us some insight.

> *It is the glory of God to conceal a thing: but the honor of kings is to search out a matter.*

I like the way *Holman Christian Standard Bible* states it: It is the glory of God to conceal a matter and the glory of the kings to *investigate* a matter. The Bible is clear from Genesis to Revelation: God has hidden powerful truths buried deep beneath the surface of the scriptures in the Bible. God does not like slothfulness or laziness; therefore, he hides things from the lazy people and the natural eye.

Our Father is a God of action. Therefore, the command is given: Seek (the verb denotes action) and you shall find, and knock (action) and it shall be open unto you! By the power of the Holy Ghost, we are going to seek the hidden treasures. We are going to knock and watch God open the mysteries up unto us. By the illumination of the Holy Ghost, we will investigate this matter. Samson went down to Timnath with his parents. Studies suggest that this city was the same city that Joshua had asked for an inheritance after they had driven the enemy out.

> When they had made an end of dividing the land for inheritance by their coasts, the children of Israel gave an inheritance to Joshua the son of Nun among them.
> According to the word of the Lord they gave him the city which he asked even Timnath-serah in mount Ephraim: and he built the city, and dwelt therein. (Judges 19:49–50)

If indeed it was the same city, then there is a very sad lesson to be learned. The city was given to Joshua and his descendants as a gift from God. As long as they were obedient to the gift giver, they were able to maintain the gift. However, we saw by the time Samson was born the city was no longer in the hands of the children of God; it's in the hands of the enemy. How did the enemy get possession of a gift given to Joshua for his obedience? Many years after the death of Joshua and the old generation that knew and served God with a pure heart died, the new generation began to worship pagan gods. Therefore, God withdrew his blessing and gave it to their enemies. Let this be a great lesson to us. If we become disobedient and take our eyes off of our Father, then the gifts or blessing given may be revoked and given to another!

Samson gave a riddle concerning his fight with a lion. The rid-dle was spiritual; therefore, the darken minds of the Philistines could not comprehend the riddle nor see the hidden powerful spiritual message. Even today there be many that claim the name of Jesus who are just as blind as the kingdom of darkness concerning deep hidden spiritual messages in the scriptures of the Bible. Darkness cannot comprehend light; therefore, we are commanded to renew our minds. Allow the Holy Ghost to illuminate it with the light of the truth, thus bringing understanding to a lost and confused mind!

The problem with many Christians is that they talk about the Father, the Son, but they are ignorant of the Holy Ghost.

Jesus said this in St. John 16:7–16:

> *Nevertheless, I tell you the truth; It is expedient for you that I go away: for if I go not away, the Comforter will not come unto you; but if I depart I will send him unto you.*
>
> *And when he is come, he will reprove the world of sin, and of righteousness, and of judgment:*
>
> *Of sin, because they believe not on me.*
>
> *Of righteousness, because I go to my Father, and ye see me no more.*
>
> *Of judgment, because the prince of this world is judged.*
>
> *I have yet many things to say unto you, but ye can-not bear them now.*
>
> *Howbeit when he, the Spirit of truth, is come, he will guide you into all truth: for he shall not speak of himself; but whatsoever he shall hear, that shall he speak: and he will show you things to come.*
>
> *He shall glorify me: for he shall receive of mine, and shall show it unto you.*
>
> *All things that the father hath are mine: therefore said I, that he shall take of mine, and shall shew it unto you.*
>
> *A little while, and ye shall not see me: and again, a little while, and ye shall see me, because I go to the Father.*

Jesus said he was going away; he was coming to the end of his earthly mission. After his resurrection, he will return back to heaven and sit on the right-hand side of his Father's throne until the appointed time in which the Father will hand him the scepter to begin his rulership over his kingdom.

He said, "Even though my mission will be done, it is better that I go."

Before Jesus came to this earth, he was a spirit. In a spirit form, he could be omnipresence (everywhere at the same time), but he made a great sacrifice for us by confining himself to a natural body.

No longer can he be everywhere at the same time, so he said, "It's best for me to go, but I will not leave you alone. I will send another. I will send the Holy Ghost who is the comforter."

The Holy Ghost is a spirit; therefore, he can be in all places at all times.

He can minister to the whole world at the same time; he will be the God of this dispensation until Jesus returned. Jesus told us the purpose of the Holy Ghost: He will guide us into all truth, he will speak whatever he hears from the Father and show it unto us, and he shall glorify us. Now that we know that the Holy Ghost is the God of this dispensation, wisdom would suggest that we develop a very close relationship with him so we can be empowered with dynamite power. When we truly understand the function of the Holy Ghost, then we will know that Jesus truly did not leave us alone. He left us a comforter: Someone who will come beside us and pick us up when we fall. Someone who will hold us when we go through painful and difficult times. Someone to protect us from all evil and to guide us into all truth!

No man can come to the Father except when the Holy Ghost draws him. The Holy Ghost seals the believer and oversees the work of salvation which begins the moment we believe in the atoning work of Jesus Christ from the foundation of this world. The Holy Ghost prays for us; he searches us and finds those hidden sins and hurts that we have concealed. The Father hears the prayers of the Holy Ghost; he then allows the enemy to set up situations that will allow these imperfections to surface. Once we have become aware of them, then it's our responsibility to pray to our Father for victory and healing. Our Father will not remove anything without our consent. We must lay it on the altar and give him permission to consume it with a cleansing fire of holiness.

If we take a close examination of Samson's battle with the lion, we will find out it's also spiritual. On the surface it just appeared to be a fight between a strong man and a young lion with the fight ending in victory for the strong man. However, hidden beneath the pages are diamonds and rubies foreshadowing and painting a pro-phetic picture of the battle between Jesus and Satan on Golgotha's hill. The first mention of this battle between the prince of peace and the prince of darkness is found in Genesis 3:15. It reads:

> *And I will put enmity between thee and the woman and between they seed and her seed; it shall bruise thy head, and thou shalt bruise his heel.*

From the beginning, God has showed us that victory over this sin nature will be accomplished by the shedding of the blood of Jesus on the cross and his triumph resurrection early Sunday morning with all power in his hands!

Samson was a type or symbolic of Jesus Christ. As he traveled with his parents, he engaged a young lion which roared against him. Notice there are two clues given to help us understand the identity of the lion. The first clue says he was a young lion and he roared. Since Samson was symbolic of Jesus Christ, then another lion was introduced here, the lion of the tribe of Judah. The lion from the tribe of Judah was an old lion because he was the alpha (beginning); therefore, he was around long before the young lion came into existence. He was the one who gave life to his most prized creation. The young lion was called by the name of Lucifer the light bearer—the one who fought against Jesus known as Michael with his angels and was defeated and kicked out to this earth.

A scripture that will give us some more insight is 1 Peter 5:8:

> *Be sober, be vigilant; because your adversary the devil, as a roaring lion* (emphasis added), *walketh about, seeking whom he may devour.*

It's plain to see that the young lion was clearly the devil. When the lion roared at Samson, the spirit of the Lord came upon him empowering him for his battle with his enemy.

> *And Jesus, when he was baptized, went up straightway out of the water: and, lo, the heavens were opened unto him, and he saw the Spirit of God descending like a dove, and lighting upon him. (Matthew 3:16)*

In chapter 4 we saw after the spirit came upon him and empowered him, he was then led by the spirit in the wilderness to do battle with the enemy.

> *The Spirit of the Lord is upon me* (emphasis added) *(John 4:18)*

These scriptures show that Samson was a type of Jesus, the old lion from the tribe of Judah empowered by the Holy Ghost to defeat the enemy. During the battle, Samson did not use any kind of weapon; he used only his body. His feet held him up strong, and his bare hands he used to rent the lion! Many years later on the cruel cross at the place of the skull known as Golgotha, we saw the same battle was no longer hidden in types but in full life. Samson had been replaced by the real Jesus and the young lion by the real devil. If indeed Samson was symbolic of Jesus, then Jesus must imitate Samson. During the battle, he could not use any weapons; he could only use his body to defeat the devil. Samson used his feet for balance and to help in his victory; the soldiers drove nails in Jesus's feet.

Fulfilling the prophecy in Genesis, *it shall bruise thy head, and thou shalt bruise his heel.* Samson then used his hands to rent the skin of the lion. The soldiers took Jesus's hands and nailed them to the cross. Using only his body just like Samson, he defeated the devil!

> *But he was wounded for our transgressions, he was bruised for our iniquities: the chastisement of our peace was upon him; and with his stripes we are healed! (Isaiah 53:5)*
> *And it was about the sixth hour, and there was a darkness all over the earth until the ninth hour.*
> *And the sun was darkened, and the veil of the temple was rent* (emphasis added) *in the midst. (Luke 23:44–45)*
> *Jesus, when he had cried again with a loud voice, yielded up the ghost.*
> *And, behold, the veil of the temple was rent in twain from the top to the bottom; and the earth did quake, and the rocks rent* (emphasis added). *(Matthew 27:50–51)*

When Adam sinned, he created a separation between God and man. Jesus came into this world to bridge the gap. Inside the temple there was an illustration of this. There was a holy place and a most holy place. They were separated by a veil that covered from the top to the bottom. The veil represented that sin had blocked man from God. Only the high priest could go behind the veil once a year and make an atonement for the sins of the people. The veil was symbolic of Jesus's skin which is supported by the book of Hebrews. At Christ's death, the veil was removed, and man can now boldly go before the Father into the holiest place themselves by the blood of Jesus.

> *Having therefore, brethren, boldness to enter into the holiest by the blood of Jesus.*
> *By a new and living way, which he has consecrated for us, through the veil, that is to say, his flesh* (emphasis added). *(Hebrews 10:19–20)*

Samson defeated his enemy by the tearing of the flesh. Jesus, the fulfillment of Samson, obtained victory over the enemy the same way, the tearing of flesh! Samson's riddle involved his victory over the lion. After the battle, he later returned the same way and discovered that honey bees had made a hive inside of the carcass of the dead lion. Samson ate some of the honey and took some to his parents to eat, but he did not tell them where it came from because he was a Nazarite. According to the Nazarite vow found in Numbers, chapters 6, he was forbidden to touch a dead body or he would become defiled. Samson gave the riddle: Out of the eater came forth meat, and out of the strong came forth sweetness.

The riddle is a physical question with spiritual implications. The thing that opposed you or was sent by the enemy to destroy you is the exact same thing God uses to empower you! I was illegally sentenced in 1994 to a twenty-year imprisonment for selling drugs. At the sentencing, I can remember telling the judge this sentence will destroy me and I will lose everything! I was wrong. It empowered me! Even though I was raised up going to church every week, it was in prison the spiritual lights came on and I discovered who my Father was. Before the prison experience, he was just a name God, but in prison he became Abba, real and personal. I enrolled into Bible colleges and took all kinds of Bible studies. I wrote my first book in prison. The title is *Why Am I in Prison?*

Only God knows how many people that book have led to the Lord for salvation. Being in prison was the worst time of my life, but the benefits from it were the best. After my release on February 20, 1999, I went from inmate Darrell Tolbert to business owner, to author of four published books (and this makes my fifth), to founder of my own church L-Jireh Ministries, Inc., to pastor, and now to Dr. Darrell Tolbert. I am a living testimony that out of the eater came forth meat! God is faithful to his word that all things, the good and the bad, will indeed be worked by him for his glory and our good. You may be facing a difficult situation, but our Father will not put on us more than we can handle.

Let's watch the Holy Ghost in action. Samson slew the lion on his way down to Timnath, but on his way back, he noticed a honey bee hive inside of the corpse. This within itself is odd because honey bees normally do not build a hive in a body or a moist place; therefore, a supernatural event had to take place in order for the carcass to be a hospital for the bees. A quick or short work had to be done! This is symbolic of the work of the Holy Ghost being done on this earth and in the saints which is recorded in Romans 9:28:

> *For he will finish the work, and cut it short in righteousness: because a short work (emphasis added) will the Lord make upon the earth.*

The bees symbolic of the Holy Ghost went into the dead body and began to work inside of it.

This is symbolic of how once we believe on Jesus the Holy Ghost comes inside of our dead body and begins his work of transformation. A hive of honey was produced inside of the dead corpse. Honey is a pure substance symbolic of the pureness of God. Honey gives energy and is the only food substance that will never spoil. This is symbolic of the Holy Ghost who empowers us and his sealing ability which seals the believer forever. The lion also symbolizes bitter situations that God has allowed to come into our life. Regardless of the bitter situation, health, financial, marriage problems, family problems, death of a loved one, loss of a job, molestation, rape, abortion, etc., if we allow the honey bees (the Holy Ghost) to do his work concerning the situation, he will turn your bitterness into something sweet!

Samson took some of the honey which came from his bitter situation and blessed his parents with it. It is symbolic of how the believer's bitter situations will be used through testimonies to bless and empower others along their Christian journey. Jesus has promised us that in this world we will have tribulations (grievous afflictions, tremendous amount of pressure, *eaters*), but be of good cheer for he has already gained our victory. He also has assured us that if we trust him in every situation, *out of the eater will come forth meat!* My plan was to end this book with that high note, but the Holy Ghost will not allow me until I illuminate another pearl hidden in the fore-shadow of Samson and Jesus.

Years after this event, we found Samson in a city called Gaza which meant strong or a goat. Like many of us, Samson had a hard time denying his flesh. If it pleases our flesh regardless if it's forbidden or not, we want it. Therefore, the command is given to crucify our flesh *daily*, thus making us victorious over the lust of the flesh. Even though called and set aside by God from the womb, he struggled in his relationship with God. I am sure we all know that struggle all too well.

Paul said it best when he said, "The things I know I shouldn't do, those are the very things I find myself doing. The things I am supposed to do are the very things I find myself not doing." Then he cried out, "Old wretched man that I am! Who shall deliver me from this great struggle?"

Then the answer comes: *I thank God through Jesus Christ our Lord!*

Gaza was a city of the enemy of Samson, the Gazites (Philistines). Forbidden places and people normally always lead to trouble. The world always has so many things to lure us into sin; therefore, the command is given for us to *be ye separate* from the world and its deadly pleasure. In Gaza, this mighty man of God's weakness was exposed. This weakness has destroyed so many men of God. Even now in 2018, it's secretly destroying about sixty-five percent of the men in the church including the pastors, bishops, prophets, and evangelists. Forty percent of the women in the church including female leader-ship also secretly struggle with it. What is this destroying secret? It's called a *sexual addiction!* Samson was not in Gaza trying to witness about his great God.

He was in Gaza having sex with a prostitute or a harlot! While in the enemy territory and enjoying the great pleasures the enemy had to offer, the enemy plots to kill him (you). The Gazites lay in wait for him so they can kill him. In my small city of Ocala, Florida, many are getting shot and killed at the clubs. The young Christians don't see the danger. They are blinded to the fact that the club is the enemy territory, and while they are enjoying the pleasure of the music, the atmosphere, and sad to say for some the alcohol, the enemy is plot-ting to kill them. This is just one of so many examples of how we allow our lust to lead us into forbidden places, and the enemy's plan is that we die right there!

> *Then went Samson to Gaza, and saw there a harlot, and went in unto her.*
> *And it was told the Gazites, saying, "Samson is come hither." And they compassed him in, and laid wait for him all night in the gate of the city, and were quiet all the night, saying, "In the morning, when it is day, we shall kill him."*
> *And Samson lay till midnight, and arose at midnight, and took the doors of the gate of the city, and the two posts, and went away with them, bar and all, and put them upon his shoulders, and carried them up to the top of a hill that is before Hebron. (Judges 16:1–3)*

Hidden in these passages are diamonds of prophetic messages concerning Jesus's death, burial, and resurrection. The first diamond: Samson came out of the city with the gates, poles, and bars on his back. The poles were wood, and the gates were made out of wood but covered in metal so the enemy couldn't burn them. They also were covered in nails so the enemy couldn't climb it. Wood and nails were being carried from the city to the top of the hill on the back of Samson. This is symbolic that one day Jesus would come out the city with a cross on his back and carry it up the hill to the top. Once at the top, he will be nailed to the wood and die for our sins. The two poles, one on either side of him, represent the two thieves that will die with him on the cross. They also represent our choice. We can choose to be on the right-hand side and receive eternal life, or we can choose to reject the salvation plan and be on the left-hand side and be condemned to eternal death!

John 19:17–18 records this:

> *And he bearing his cross went forth into a place called the place of the skull, which is called in the Hebrew Golgotha: Where they crucified him, and two other with him, on either side one, and Jesus in the midst.*

The second diamond: The enemy waited all night watching Samson, symbolic of the soldiers watching Jesus's tomb all night. His enemies thought the locked gates could keep Samson locked inside just like the devil, and the Jewish leaders thought the sealed tomb and soldiers could hold Jesus inside. Early in the morning, Samson burst forth with the gates and carried them victoriously to the top, high above the earth so all his enemies could see! Inside the Bible, the word "hell" is sometimes the meaning for the grave depending on the context in which the word is used.

> *I said in the cutting off of my days, I shall go to the gates of the grave: I am deprived of the residue of my years. (Isaiah 38:10)*

Like Samson, early Sunday morning, Jesus burst forth from the graves with the gates of hell victoriously and was raised high above the earth so all his enemies could see.

> *And when he had spoken these things, while they beheld, he was taken up; and a cloud received him out of their sight. (Acts 1:9)*
> *Who being the brightness of his glory, and the express image of his person, and upholding all things by the word of his power, when he had by himself purged our sins, sat down at the right hand of the Majesty on high. (Hebrews 1:3)*

Samson was just like all of us. Once delivered from one situa-tion, we go right back to it or get trapped in another situation. The fatal mistakes that many Christians make are to underestimate the power of the enemy and to be in denial about their own weaknesses and strongholds. Our talk is more powerful than our walk. We have more head knowledge than we have spiritual heart knowledge. This means we may know a scripture, but the application of the word is far from us—more shouting in church than obedience outside of the church, more talking about Jesus than being like Jesus, and more talking about the kingdom than being the kingdom. Samson even though called to deliver others was trapped himself. It sounds just like us. Inside of him, there was a battle going on, the spirit warring against the flesh, and his action showed that he was losing the battle inside of his mind.

Oftentimes we focus on the behavior but are blinded to what caused the action, the mind! That's why the Holy Ghost through the Apostle Paul wrote in Romans 12:20:

> *And be not conformed to this world: but be ye transformed by the renewing of your mind, that ye may prove what is that good, and acceptable, and perfect, will of God.*

Samson even though chosen by God from birth like all of us had to learn the key to victory and salvation. That key is called obedience! Many do not know that the majority of the time obedience is learned through our suffering. The Bible is clear on that point:

> *Though he were a Son, yet learned he obedience by the things which he suffered. (Hebrews 5:8)*

Note the word "learned." It denotes a process achieved through study or in this case experience.

Suffering for Jesus's sake creates character. It kills off the lust for the world and leaves a deep desire for a closer relationship with our Father, our elder brother Jesus Christ, and our teacher the Holy Ghost. Suffering proves who you really are. It's easy to shout and praise God when all is well, but the true sign of a life devoted to the Father is being able to shout and praise him while still being obedient as you are suffering for the gospel's sake. Let me point this truth out: All of our suffering is not a result of the gospel. The majority of the time it's the result of disobedience as we will see as I continue with the story of Samson. After breaking free from the city, we didn't find Samson somewhere praising the Lord for being delivered from his enemies. We didn't find this great man chosen by God to deliver his people rededicating his life and focusing on his God-given mission.

We found this man of God in another Philistine city, in love with another Philistine woman that's forbidden by God! Samson seemed to have great love for these forbidden women. His first wife, the prostitutes, and now Delilah. Samson seemed to have a lust issue. He could defeat the men on the outside, but he hadn't learned how to conquer the man on the inside! Jesus is clear that it's not what's on the outside that defiles you. It is what's on the inside that manifests on the outside that destroys you!

> *And it came to pass afterward, that he loved a woman in the valley of Sorek, whose name was Delilah. (Judges 16:4)*

Sorek is the name of the Philistine city, and the name means choice vine, valley of the fertile spot which drains the western Judean hills and, flowing by Makkedah and Jabneel, falls into the sea some eight miles south of Joppa. Interestingly the city drained water from one place and sent it to another. Unknown to Samson, this was the city that his *strength* will be drained!

The name Delilah has many meanings. In Arabic the name means *night*. In Hebrew, the meaning of the name is amorous, delight, languishing, or temptress. It's the last meaning that I want to focus on. Temptress means a woman who tempts someone to do something, typically a sexually attractive woman who sets out to allure or seduce someone. Samson's first wife withheld him from his mission, the prostitutes in Gaza defiled him, and now Delilah was about to bring him down low! We fail to realize that sin is not our friend even though it has pleasures that may last for a season. It's main purpose is to destroy us in the end! Samson escaped the enemy in Gaza, but the enemy didn't give up. He knew a victory today doesn't guarantee a victory tomorrow. The Arabic name meaning darkness sheds some light of this great battle.

The kingdom of darkness Delilah and the Philistines against the kingdom of light Samson: Notice the devil used darkness to lure Samson to his destruction. He knew what Samson loved. He knows what you love also. He knows the things that are hidden in our hearts.

That's why King David said, *Create in me a clean heart, O God; and renew a right spirit within me (Psalm 51:10).*

Samson's spirit had become contaminated through his association and disobedience, thus giving the enemy power to exploit his weakness. Even though Delilah was the instrument used by the enemy to find Samson's weakness, she was not the cause of his fall. I mentioned this earlier. It was the things inside of him that defeated him.

> *But every man is tempted when he is drawn away of his own lust and enticed.*
> *Then when lust hath conceived, it bringeth forth sin: and sin, when it is finished, bringeth forth death. (James 1:14–15)*

Samson was under pressure from Delilah daily unto the point that his spirit was vexed causing him to reveal his secret. The devil is rentless in his pursuit to destroy us; therefore, we are commanded to put on and keep on the whole armor of God so we can stand against the attacks of our enemy. The lords of the Philistines revealed the intent of the devil, his evil desire for all of us.

> *And the lords of the Philistines came up unto her, and said unto her, "Entice him, and see wherein his great strength lieth, and by what means we may prevail against him, that we may bind him to afflict him: and we will give thee every one of us eleven hundred pieces of silver." (Judges 16:5)*

Note the three things the enemy wants to do to us: *prevail against us, bind, and afflict!* Let's examine these three methods used by the enemy real closely.

*Prevail:* Prove more powerful than opposing forces, be victorious. The devil wants to try and prove that he is more powerful than the God we serve. He wants us to doubt that *greater is he that's in us* than he is in the world. He was victorious over Adam and Eve. He is victorious over us when we operate in the old man and fail to use the power given to us; however, he has never been victorious over our Father, his Son, nor the Holy Ghost! My victory over the devil for salvation wasn't based on what I did but rather what Jesus did on the cross over two thousand years ago. He walked out the tomb early Sunday morning victorious, and as a believer I share in that same victory over the devil. Since I am in Jesus when Jesus defeated him on the cross, I defeated him on the cross. This is a truth that the enemy fights hard to blind our minds to. If we ever grasp this concept of victory, then it will be hard for the enemy to defeat a person who knows they are victorious over all their enemies!

*Bind*: Tie or fasten something tightly, to prevent free movement, restrain, or hold in bondage. God has freed us in the spiritual realm from all bondage; however, the enemy knows that all disobedience is sin. He also knows that sin is like a rope. It will bind us tight, thus taking away our freedom and hindering us from going higher or getting closer to our Father. Sin and weight can hold us tight and keep us trapped. Therefore, we are commanded to *lay aside every weight and the sin which doth so easily beset us, and let us run with patience the race that is set before us.* The enemy uses everything that goes against righteousness to entice us so he can bind us tight by ropes of sin!

*Afflict*: Cause pain or suffering to; affect or trouble greatly or grievously. In order for Jesus to save us, the enemy afflicted him and caused him great pain by the thirty-nine lashes from the whip that ripped his back into pieces, spit in the face, slap to the face, painful crown of thorns forced down upon his head, and lastly agoniz-ing nails in his hands and feet. The enemy afflicts pain to stop us from moving forward. Pain will test your faith and even cause you to doubt the promises of God. Pain has caused many to walk away from the faith. When Job was faced with pain, his wife told him to curse his God and die, but Job rebuked her by saying, "You sound like a foolish woman." The million-dollar question is this, why does our father allow the devil to afflict his children? On the surface it seems so unfair. Our natural thought is this: If God so loved us, then he should protect us from affliction and not allow it to happen. The answer can be found in Exodus 1:12:

> *But the more they afflicted them, the more they multiplied and grew* (emphasis added).

The enemy does it for our harm, but God allows it for our spiritual growth!

Delilah was paid eleven hundred pieces of silver by each of the five lords which equaled five thousand five hundred shekels of silver nearly two talents. One author estimates the amount in our currency to equal to $89,641.00. Therefore, she was paid a great sum of money to betray Samson. The large amount showed the great desire they had to defeat him and destroy him. The devil still has this great desire to defeat and destroy us. He has the Malcolm X mentality: *by any means necessary!* Samson gave up the secret, but even Samson was blinded to the true source of his strength. He thought it was in his hair, but the truth of the matter is that his strength is in his obedience. God said not to cut his hair, and as long as he obeyed that command, he had strength. But disobedience to that command caused him to lose his strength.

That is true for all believers. God is the source of our power, and if we are separated from the vein (God), then we become powerless. The Bible is clear: Our sins or disobedience has separated us from God. Samson gave in, but here is the key thing that jumps out at me: He thought even in his disobedience God will always be there protecting him. He laid his head in the lap of Delilah, the one whom he thought loved him. I preached a sermon once with the title of "Watch Where You Lay Your Head"! Once his hair was cut, the hedge of protection was removed. The Bible records some sad words:

*Samson said, I will go out as times before.*

*But he did not know the Lord has departed from him!* If we continue in sin, judgment will soon follow. The enemy moved in on him and bound him tight. To his horror he found himself unable to break free. They put his eyes out, thus limiting his ability to fight back. A blind man is useless as a warrior because he cannot see the attacks of the enemy.

This is true for the spiritual eyes also; the devil works in the exact same way!

*He has blinded their eyes and hardened their hearts, lest they see with their eyes, and understand with their heart, and turn, and I would heal them. (John 12:40)*
*In whom the god of this world hath blinded the minds of them which believe not, lest the light of the glorious*

*gospel of Christ, who is the image of God, should shine unto them. (2 Corinthians 4:4)*

As believers, we fail to understand that sin is darkness and darkness is bondage. If you are blind, then you are at the mercy of the individual that's leading you. If you are being led by the Holy Ghost, then that's an awesome thing; but if you are being led by the devil, then you are in a world of trouble. Samson was about to learn this lesson the hard way, a lesson that could have been avoided if he would have been fully committed to God.

Samson played with sin and thought he could break free as always. So many of us have the same mind frame. We think we can continue to willfully sin and God will always forgive us. However, like Samson, one day we will be a victim of a rude awakening! We will find ourselves trapped and unable to break free.

> *For if we sin willfully after that we have received the knowledge of the truth, there remaineth no more sacrifice for sins.*
> *But a certain fearful looking for of judgment and fiery indignation, which shall devour the adversaries. (Hebrews 10:26–27)*
> *Of how much sorer punishment, suppose ye, shall he be thought worthy, who hath trodden under foot the Son of God, and hath counted the blood of the covenant, wherewith he was sanctified, an unholy thing, and hath done despite unto the spirit of grace?*
> *For we know him that hath said, "Vengeance belongeth unto me, I will recompense," saith the Lord. And again, The Lord shall judge his people.*
> *It is a fearful thing to fall into the hands of the living God. (Hebrews 10:29–31)*

Once bound by the enemy, they took him back to the exact same place he had escaped from—the same place where he was visiting prostitutes and contaminating his spirit. This jumps out at me; the scriptures said they brought him down to Gaza. Sin will bring you down every time! There is no spiritual elevation in a lifestyle of sin. It only travels in one direction, and that's downward. Gaza means strong or strong city. It was here where he was held in prison. Note the word "strong." It is symbolic of the strongholds we have in our life. These strongholds are sins that hold us tight in a spiritual prison. Sexual sins lead to sexual ties which bind us to the individual long after we desire to be free and move on in life. They placed him in the prison house and forced him to grind. Sent into this world to be used by God for his glorious work, now he was a prisoner being used by the enemy to do his lowly work!

As a man who had been in prison, I have an idea of the things that probably went through Samson's mind. You take a trip back into the past. Everything that you know concerning right and wrongs comes flooding back to you. All the warnings that God had given to you come back—people who tried to encourage you to focus on God, their faces come floating through your mind. Then you think of how great you could have been, and then depression sets in because to you your current situations prove you are a failure in life. You beat yourself up and begin on the "if I would have done this or that, then I won't be in this situation." Self-pity sets in. The greater your life was before the fall, the greater the self-condemnation. However, God had not abandoned him. I am a living witness that God is at work inside of the prisons transforming sinners into saints for his glory.

As the long hard days went by, something began to happen that the enemy wasn't paying attention to: his hair was growing back. It is symbolic of his relationship with God growing every day. We may fall down, but grace allows us to get back up. If we confess our sins and change our ways, God is faithful and just to forgive us and cleanse us from all unrighteousness. The devil may win some battles during this Christian journey, but because of Jesus's death, burial, and resurrection, we have already won the war! Disobedience will not abort God's divine purpose in our lives. God sent Samson into this world to be a deliverer and to set the Jews free. As a result of being blind and in prison, it seemed as if God's plan for his life had become void.

But the word of God declares, "My spirit shall go forth from me and it shall not come back void. It will accomplish the purpose it was sent forth to do."

There came a day when the Philistines gathered themselves together to worship and offer up sacrifices to their god, Dagon, which was an ancient Levantine (Canaanite) deity. He appeared to have been worshipped as a fertility god in Ebla and Ugarit and among the Amorites. The Hebrew Bible mentions him as the national god of the Philistines with temples at Ashdod and elsewhere in Gaza.

*Then the lords of the Philistines gathered them together for to offer a great sacrifice unto Dagon their god, and to rejoice: for they said, "Our god hath delivered Samson our enemy into our hand."*

*And when the people saw him, they praised their god: for they said, "Our god hath delivered into our hands our enemy, and the destroyer of our country, which slew many of us."*

*And it came to pass, when their hearts were merry, that they said, "Call for Samson, that he may make us sport." And they called for Samson out of the prison house; and he made them sport: and they set him between the pillars.*

*And Samson said unto the lad that held him by the hand, "Suffer me that I may feel the pillars whereupon the house standeth, that I may lean upon them."*

*Now the house was full of men and women; and all the lords of the Philistines were there; and there were upon the roof about three thousand men and women, that beheld while Samson made sport.*

*And Samson called unto the Lord, and said, "O Lord God, remember me, I pray thee, and strengthen me, I pray thee, only this once, O God, that I may be at once avenged of the Philistines for my two eyes."*

*And Samson took hold of the two middle pillars upon which the house stood, and on which it was borne up, of the one with his right hand, and of the other with his left.*

*And Samson said, "Let me die with the Philistines." And he bowed himself with all his might; and the house fell upon the lords, and upon all the people that were within. So the dead which he slew at his death were more than they which he slew in his life.*

*Then his brethren and all the house of his father came down, and took him, and brought him up, and buried*

*him between Zorah and Eshtaol in the burying place of
Manoah his father. And he hath judged Israel twenty
years. (Judges 16:23–31)*

As I mentioned before, Samson is symbolic of Jesus Christ, so
hidden inside of this story are some hidden diamonds of foreshadows
concerning the divine purpose and death of Jesus on the cross.
Remember earlier I mentioned there were five Philistine lords. I will
bring out the hidden message in the number 5 concerning Jesus, but
first I want to focus on the lies of the lords to keep the people blinded
to the truth of the real God. We know they paid money to Delilah to
obtain Samson's source of strength. However, during the feast, they told
the people victory was obtained by the power of Dagon. This enforced
the people's belief in a dead powerless pagan god, thus holding them
captive in darkness and death.

Unknown to the Philistines, the true God was about to deliver his
people from their power. His purpose for sending Samson into this
world had not changed, and God was about to bring judgment upon
them for their rejection of him for a god made with human hands. The
five lords called for Samson. "Five" has several meanings, but the one I
want to focus on is this: grace. Grace came by Jesus on the cross. There
are five lords symbolic of the five piercings Jesus had on his body as a
result of his death on the cross—hole in the right hand, the left hand,
the right foot, the left foot, and his side. So we can clearly see from the
five lords a prophetic picture of Jesus's death on the cross years later.

They made a very bad mistake by sending for Samson. They
brought him out for the purpose of exalting their god and making a
mockery out of him and his God. However, they were ignorant to this
fact found in Galatians 6:7:

> *Be not deceived; God is not mocked: for whatsoever a man
> soweth, that shall he also reap.*

Samson came out being led by a lad. The irony in this is the once
great leader is now being led. Our leading of ourselves always led to
destruction and harm, but those who follow the good shepherd always
find themselves on solid ground safe and sound. Samson had been in
Gaza before hanging out with the prostitutes; therefore, he knew the
layout of the city and the buildings. After entertaining the crowd, he

asked the lad to put his hands on the pillars that supported the main house.

Oftentimes we are compared to a house. The question becomes, what foundation is your house built on? Is Jesus the chief cornerstone that supports your faith? Our God will allow the kingdom of darkness to test our house so we can see what foundation it is set upon. Sadly, we sometimes see that it's built on sand, and when tested it falls and crumbles into pieces. Samson saw his opportunity to fulfill his divine appointment. He knew the pillars were the main support to the house. Once his hands were upon the pillars, he prayed to the source of his strength. Being in prison had caused him to focus on his destiny and his God-given purpose. Before he was captured, life was about him and the things that pleased him well. He refused to die to self so he could live for God. How many of us are guilty of the same thing?

Could it be the reason why you are experiencing hardship is because your life is all about you? Yes, you go to church and go through the motion of church, but in your private life after church is over, God takes the backseat. Pie your life out and see how much time is given to our Father. If we will be honest about it, God gets the smallest piece of the pie! As a result of this, we fall under pressure often from the kingdom of darkness. It is not until we die we begin to live. Life begins with death to ourselves. Jesus said that a seed must fall to the ground and die before it begins to sprout. Samson was in the position that God wants all of us to be in, that is, life being about him even if we die doing his will! His prayer didn't consist of saving his life but rather giving him the power one more time not to exalt himself but to destroy his enemies.

This prayer is in the will of God. This is why God sent him into the world. He stood in the middle between the two pillars. His left hand was on one and his right hand was on the other. This stretched-out position reveals unseen diamonds. Hidden inside of it is Jesus and the way he died on the cross. One thief was on the right and the other thief on the left, and Jesus had his arms stretched out wide. He pushed with all his might, and the Philistine kingdom came falling down in a loud crumbling and rumbling. At Jesus's death, the king-dom of darkness crumbled and the earth rumbled as it's shaken by an earthquake. No man took Samson's life. He freely laid it down to defeat his enemy and to free his people. Likewise, no man took Jesus's life. He freely laid it down to defeat his enemy and to free the world from the power of the devil.

At Samson's death, he defeated more of his enemies than during his life. At Jesus's death he saved more people than when he was alive. Death to ourselves always produced a greater harvest for the kingdom of light. Samson's family came to Gaza to retrieve his body from the ruins and took him back to the place of his birth. Likewise, at Jesus's death, his brethren came for his body and buried him among the rich, symbolic of his position before coming to earth which is recorded in 2 Corinthians 8:9:

> *For ye know the grace of our Lord Jesus Christ, that, though he was rich, yet for your sakes he became poor, that ye through his poverty might be rich.*

When I look at the life of Samson, it really makes me want to cry. It didn't have to end with his eyes being put out and his death with his enemies.

If he would have sold out to God, he may have lived a long victorious life over his enemies only to be defeated by old age. When I look at the six years and five months I spent in prison, the reality of it is this: Even though God worked it out for his glory and my good, it still could have been avoided by making the right choices. We carry a lot of unnecessary scars on our bodies and in our souls. Many would have been avoided if only we had obeyed what we know to be right instead of doing the things that please us well. There is a way that seem right unto us, but it's a way filled with pain and heartache and that ends in destruction.

In closing I encourage you to keep the faith and hold on to God's unchanging hand! Weeping may endure for a night, but joy will come in the morning. It doesn't matter how out of control this world may seem. Our Father is still in control. The eater will come, but our God has promised us that all things (good and evil) will work together for our good and His glory. Out of the eater (adverse situations) will come forth meat (victory and strength to move forward) in our journey toward heaven! Our bad choices do not negate the purpose God has for our lives!

# EPILOGUE

The Holy Ghost has done it again. He has used a nobody like me to illuminate hidden treasures in the Bible. I want to thank my wife, Kathy, for the love and support while I worked on this book. I want to thank my daughter, L-Jireh, for her patience. There were times when she wanted me to play with her, but I was engaged in this book. I thank my Father in heaven for giving me this gift to write books. My thoughts are toward the late Dr. Bishop Delores Ward, my aunt. When I needed spiritual guidance, she was there. She was looking forward to reading this book. You are truly missed by me.

All scriptures used in this book was taken from the *King James Bible* unless otherwise stated.

Genesis 1:3, Exodus 14:5–9,21–28, Genesis 15:13–16, Deuteronomy 7:22, Numbers 13:25–33, Deuteronomy 8:2–3, Judges 2:6–10, Judges 2:11–19, Judges 13:1–7, Judges 13:17–18, Isaiah 9:6–7, Judges 13:19–22, Psalms 84:11, Malachi 4:2, Matthew 10:37, Judges 14:5–14, Proverbs 25:2, Judges 19:49–50, John 16:7–16, Genesis 3:15, 1 Peter 5:8, John 4:18, Isaiah 53:5, Luke 23:44–45, Matthew 27:50–51, Hebrews 10:19–20, Romans 8:28, Judges 16:1–3, John 19:17–18, Isaiah 38:10, Acts 1:9, Hebrews 1:3, Psalms 51:10, James 1:14–15, Judges 16:5, Exodus 1:12, John 12:40, 2 Corinthians 4:4, Hebrews 10:26–27, 29-31, Judges 16:23–31, Galatians 6:7, 2 Corinthians 8:9

# ABOUT THE AUTHOR

Dr. Darrell Tolbert is married to Kathy Fowler Tolbert. He has five children all grown except one: Nathan, Durrell, Darreka, Jalecia, and L-Jireh. He is the founder and pastor of L-Jireh Ministries, Inc., a non-denominational church. He is the author of four more published books: *Why Am I in Prison?*, *Until God's Purpose Is Accomplished!*, *Raider's of the Tombs!*, and *The Woman at the Well!* These books are available on Amazon. He was enrolled in the American Bible Academy, was a graduate of the United Bible Institute, has a master's degree in theology from the College of The Open Bible, and has a doctorate degree in theology from the National School of Theology. He is currently enrolled in the College of The Open Bible working on a doctorate degree in divinity. He also does prison and street ministry. He is the co-founder of a Bible college in Hyderabad, India, for pastors. You can learn more about him from his website www.L-Jirehministries. com. For speaking engagements, call 352-361-8473.